The
Five
Stages
of
Grief

by Linda Pastan

A Perfect Circle of Sun

On the Way to the Zoo

Aspects of Eve

The Five Stages of Grief
   Winner of the di Castagnola Award

The Five Stages of Grief

Poems
by
Linda
Pastan

W · W · Norton & Company · Inc ·
New York

I would like to thank the following magazines in which some of these poems first appeared: *The Agni Review; The Antioch Review; The American Scholar; Apocalypse; The Atlantic Monthly; Black Box; The Blacksmith; The Chicago Review; Choice; Dryad Gargoyle; The Iowa Review; Mademoiselle; Ms.; Moment; The Nation; The New Yorker; The New Republic; The Ohio Review; The Ontario Review; Plough-shares; Poetry; Poetry Now; Prairie Schooner; SCOP; Southern Poetry Review; Thistle; Three Rivers Poetry Journal; The Washingtonian.* "Paperweight" was part of the cold Mountain Press Poetry Post Card Series. "Poet" was part of a Post Card Series edited by Marcia Falk.

Certain portions of this work copyright © 1977 by *The New Yorker*, the United Chapters of Phi Beta Kappa, Dryad Press, the Modern Poetry Association, University of Nebraska Press, Three Rivers Press, Ernest and Cis Stefanik, the editors of *The Ohio Review*, Ploughshares Inc., Richard Peabody, Jr.; © 1976 by the Agni Review, the Atlantic Monthly Company, Gail Mazur, University of Iowa, Washington Magazine, Inc.; © 1975 by the Condé Nast Publications, Inc., Continuity, Inc., the Nation Associates, Inc., E. V. Griffith, Linda Pastan; © 1973, by *Southern Poetry Review*, Linda Pastan.

Library of Congress Cataloging in Publication Data

Pastan, Linda.
  The five stages of grief.

  I. Title.
PS 3566.A775F5   811'.5'4   77–22157

ISBN 0 393 04489 0 cloth edition
ISBN 0 393 04494 7 paper edition

 2 3 4 5 6 7 8 9 0

Again, for Ira

Contents

You may my glories and my state depose,
But not my griefs. Still am I king of those.

William Shakespeare,
King Richard the Second

1. denial

Funerary Tower: Han Dynasty
"The meaning of the figures carrying babies in their arms is not clear."

In this season of salt
leaves drop away
revealing the structure
of the trees.

Good bones,
as my father would say
drawing the hair from my face.
I'd pull impatiently away.

Today we visit my father's grave.
My mother housekeeps, with trowel
among the stones,
already at home here.

Impatient, even at forty
I hurry her home.
We carry our childhoods
in our arms.

After

After the month
in Sicily,
the ocean's edge unravelling
around our own
volcanic knees;
after the dark plums
that throbbed like fairy tale hearts
in the woodsman's basket;
the voyage in another's arms
where we were innocent
as tourists
visiting familiar landscapes
for the first time

we come back
to our old lives
as to a heap of clothes
we have left in our closet,
and either they have shrunk
or we have grown fat
on the risen cream
of ease.
But soon our old possessions
cry out
like artifacts
not to be buried yet.
We are claimed

by our dishes, by their need
to be washed and dried
and put away;
by our mattress which like a pliant wife
has shaped itself
to our remembered bodies.
And at the edge of the grass
our deaths wait like domestic animals.
They have been there all along,
patient and loving.
We must hurry
or we may miss them
in the swelling dark.

Egg

In this kingdom
the sun never sets;
under the pale oval
of the sky
there seems no way in
or out,
and though there is a sea here
there is no tide.

For the egg itself
is a moon
glowing faintly
in the galaxy of the barn,
safe but for the spoon's
ominous thunder,
the first delicate crack
of lightning.

in the shadows: for Mark Strand

it is
a matter
of light

we rise in darkness
go down
in darkness

in the dusk
we remember
what we had almost forgotten

by starlight
we suspect
what we almost knew

there is truth in the shadows
moving like water
to the tug of the moon

only when darkness
is splintered
by the fierce blow of the sun

do we open our eyes
finally
and dream

Voices

Joan heard voices,
and she burned for it.
Driving through the dark
I write poems.
Last night I drove through
a stop sign, pondering
line breaks.
When I explained
the policeman nodded,
then he gave me
a ticket.
Someone who knows told me
writers have fifteen years:
then comes repetition,
even madness.
Like Midas, I guess
everything we touch turns
to a poem—
when the spell is on.
But think of the poet after that
touching the trees
he's always touched,
but this time nothing happens.
Picture him rushing from trunk
to trunk, bruising
his hands on the rough bark.
Only five years left.
Sometimes I bury
my poems in the garden,
saving them
for the cold days ahead.
One way or another
you burn for it.

Adultery

"Between the motion/And the act/Falls the shadow . . ."
T. S. Eliot

What does it mean,
this coming together at noon
when there are no shadows
to tug like the past at our heels
or to beat a dark path ahead of us
which we must follow?
True, my hair shadows your face.
But when we stand this way
at this hour
not even Euclid could take our measure—
we are a pillar of pure heat.
And if someone should mention to us
how Saint Peter healed
with his shadow
though we know pain
we would hardly listen.

Argument

When I describe
your absence,
here you are
with me
on the white sheets
of paper.

Last week
on real sheets
I covered my ears against
your talk of leaving—
there was no such talk.
It is an old argument:

the tree falling
in the forest
with no one
to hear.
Now I am lost
in that forest.

Waking In Norway

1

Caught by daylight
the troll
is turned into
a stone.
The child I am
wakens afraid
in the body of a woman.
And what of the tree?
And what of the chair?
The sun struggles up
from the fjord
as I struggle
out of sleep
into a strange
country.

2

This is my ninth journey.
I have used up the others
as the cat has,
never knowing where I am
until I have left.
Memory will turn
its dark pages back,
but now as in a dream
I speak a language
no one speaks,
move among
mountains
where rivulets start
their frozen
descent,
melting absently
halfway down.

3

At home morning
is still remote;
this brightness
this rippling of light
touches my hand
but those I've left
sleep, wrapped

in the darkness
the small night
I carry with me.

4

So many journeys,
the old man says.
So many children leaving
for Oslo.
They will forget
that to live
through the winter
they had to go down
to the sea for salt.
And they called the road
The Salt Road,
never looking back,
passing these roofs
made of sod
where the grass has grown
all night,
as hair grows
on the heads of the dead
we leave behind.

Self Portrait at 44

How friendly
my failures have become,
how undemanding.
Scraping chairs across the room
they sit down next to me
like family almost,
and indeed we have grown
to look alike.
One of them always puts
a log on the fire
and though it's wet
and fouls the room
I am warm for awhile,
and drunk with yawning
I sometimes fall asleep
sitting up.

2. anger

Poem On A Line By Robert Creeley

The night my surgeon father
slammed from me
in rage,
he wore a scrub suit
of leaf green—and he
an old stump,
axed and buried now
for six years.
All men are babies,
my mother said.

Surgeons are babies
that grow on trees
small, sour apples in green masks
stethoscopes twisting like vines
from their pockets
to catch the pulse
of our betrayals.
See me lift my skirt
among strangers
to show them my scar.

In The Old Guerilla War

In the old guerilla war
between father and son
I am the no man's land.
When the moon shows
over my scorched breast
they fire across me.
If a bullet ricochets
and I bleed,
they say it is my time
of month.
Sometimes I iron
handkerchiefs
into flags of truce,
hide them in pockets;
or humming, I roll socks
instead of bandages.
Then we sit down together
breaking only bread.
The family tree
shades us, the snipers
waiting in its branches
sleep between green leaves.
I think of the elm
sending its roots
like spies underground
through any rough terrain
in search of water;
or Noah sending out the dove
to find land.
Only survive long enough;
the triggers
will rust into rings
around both their fingers.
I will be a field
where all the flowers
on my housedress
bloom at once.

Memorial Banquet: for Gordon

After the soup
a woman said to me
"I consider his death
unacceptable"
as if it were a package,
and I had accepted it.
Look, I wanted to say back
I'm only here by marriage,
I hardly knew him.
Our friendship was pure
potential: a single afternoon
watching the scenery.
That day the trees said
winter but meant spring.
And he said spring   spring   summer.
But already the first flakes
were falling inside his head;
the blizzard was on its way
that would snow him in,
would blow his eyes shut.
Already this banquet
was on the schedule.

My Grandmother

My grandmother
of the bitter mouth
and the capable hands
taught us how long you can live
without love
and be forgiven
and never forgive.
She married knowingly,
at her father's bidding,
the wrong man.
And though she called
each granddaughter "shaneh madeleh"
which means "lovely girl,"
when my cousin married
a gentile boy for love
she covered her mirrors
as for death:
for seven days
she didn't see
her once beautiful face
wasted in the glass.

Soup

"A rich man's soup—and all from a few stones."
Marcia Brown, *Stone Soup*

If your heart feels
like a stone
make stone soup of it.
Borrow the parsley
from a younger woman's garden.
Dig up a bunch of rigid carrots.
Your own icebox is full
of the homelier vegetables.
Now cry into the pot.
When he comes home
serve him a steaming bowlful.
Then watch him as he bites
into the stone.

Marks

My husband gives me an A
for last night's supper,
an incomplete for my ironing,
a B plus in bed.
My son says I am average,
an average mother, but if
I put my mind to it
I could improve.
My daughter believes
in Pass/Fail and tells me
I pass. Wait 'til they learn
I'm dropping out.

Death Is The Final Consumer

Ask Ralph Nader:
the truth is
life is a carcinogen,
that's why I've tried
so many times
to give it up.
At first I tried
a little at a time:
never staring at sunsets,
making love
with the lights out.
Then I tried cold turkey,
but when I stood
on the roof to jump,
television aerials
gleamed like crucifixes,
chimneys sent up signals
of smoke I couldn't ignore.
But now we're gunning
for each other
me and life
with registered handguns.
Only death is a hundred percent
pure—it's incorruptible.
Ask Ralph Nader.

It Is Raining On The House Of Anne Frank

It is raining on the house
of Anne Frank
and on the tourists
herded together under the shadow
of their umbrellas,
on the perfectly silent
tourists who would rather be
somewhere else
but who wait here on stairs
so steep they must rise
to some occasion
high in the empty loft,
in the quaint toilet,
in the skeleton
of a kitchen
or on the map—
each of its arrows
a barb of wire—
with all the dates, the expulsions,
the forbidding shapes
of continents.
And across Amsterdam it is raining
on the Van Gogh Museum
where we will hurry next
to see how someone else
could find the pure
center of light
within the dark circle
of his demons.

Exeunt Omnes

Let everything happen
off-stage
Leave me
with the scenery:
with the stream which this morning
is all surfaces;
the hills which alter
no more than their colors;
with the old passion
of the seasons
changing.
Let the only dialogue
be between hawk and crow
in their innocent
murderous play.
Go away,
all of you.

3. bargaining

A Short History Of Judaic Thought In The Twentieth Century

The rabbis wrote:
although it is forbidden
to touch a dying person,
nevertheless, if the house
catches fire
he must be removed
from the house.

Barbaric!
I say,
and whom may I touch then,
aren't we all
dying?

You smile
your old negotiator's smile
and ask:
but aren't all our houses
burning?

Ice Age

The Pterosaurus on the roof
spreads its ghostly wings
to shelter us.
In the thermometers
the mercury slides
to the bottom
making pools of silver—
we skate on them.
The world's weather is growing cold.
Already glaciers are moving
towards Maryland
where just now a light snow
started to fall,
and women are already knitting mufflers
which will not be thick enough
to warm our throats.
The snow is vague at the windows,
an early symptom.
Later the flakes will multiply,
the house will be wrapped
in a winding sheet of snow
snow like snuff in the nostrils,
like ash in the chimneys.
The children will build a house of snow
and disappear inside it.
Now wooly bears grow thick, black
mourning bands,
carrots burrow deep.
I have heard of miller moths
breaking into houses,
have seen my own breath ice mirrors—
they will need no other covering.
We must learn
the cold lessons
the dinosaurs learned:
to freeze magnified
in someone else's history;
to leave our bones behind.

Chagall

It is snowing
fiddle notes
on the village of Vitebsk
where brides float up
like the wicks
of sabbath candles.
In the kitchens
the dough cries out
to be braided,
or is it the hair
of the youngest daughter
newly washed
in ochre?

Fresco

In Masaccio's "Expulsion
From the Garden"
how benign the angel seems,
like a good civil servant
he is merely enforcing
the rules. I remember
these faces from Fine Arts 13.
I was young enough then
to think that the loss of innocence
was just about Sex.
Now I see Eve covering
her breasts with her hands
and I know it is not to hide them
but only to keep them
from all she must know
is to follow
from Abel on one,
Cain on the other.

March

It is a season
of divorce.
February ends
abruptly.
Oak trees which have fiercely
held to their leaves
all winter
suddenly
let go.
Our friends
tear apart.

We married so young.
I think of pictures
of Asian princes
betrothed at five,
their enormous eyes
accepting anything.

In the woods
dogs nose among emptied burrows,
bark at the silence.
Don't leave now.
We have almost
survived
our lives.

Poet

At his right hand
silence;
at his left hand
silence;
ahead of him
the yahrzeit glass;
behind him
silence;
and above his head
all the letters of the alphabet
to choose from.

"Physics For Poets"

Electrons move
around their nucleus
like moths circling a light
or earth the sun.
I see the iris
push up from earth
against gravity.
At night is it the wind
or waves, sound or motion
that rocks this house
propelling us
to sleep? Dreams
revolve around our heads—
dark planets,
dark questions;
is God so stingy with form?
Is each of us no more than metaphor
for something else?
We slip back
to our chemical selves
holding our arms out to each other
like valences
sensing our power
to combine.

Terminal

For every departure
there is an arrival.
It is the law of the axe
whose handle was a tree.
It is the secret
the fire caves in upon
whose smoke disappears
along its own trail.
The leaves push off again—
a whole fleet of small sails
and no one knows where they land.
Children wave from train windows
their years growing heavy
on their backs.
But somewhere a cloud is forming
that will flower here
in petals of snow,
and light from a star
that started towards us
a million years ago
arrives at last.

Return

Instinctive as swallows
the migratory children
return at Christmas,
strewing the roads
with their brief colors,
moving like the weather
from south to north,
from west to east.

It is November,
these flakes at the window
are only leaves.
But already the ritual
readies itself,
it is a birth we prepare for,
the homing
of children.

whom do you visualize as your reader?

the humanities 5 section man
who has been sharpening
his red pencil
these twenty years

my mother
who suspected me
of such thoughts
all along

the running back
who after the last touchdown
reads my poems by his locker
instead of the sports page

Bicentennial Winter

The only revolution is among the oaks
here in the woods;
their mutinous leaves
refuse to fall, despite
the laws of season
and of gravity.
Red-coated cardinals hide
among those leaves.
Red bird, cold weather
the farmers say.
Know us by our myths.
I think of the mutinous
Puritans who taught us
that all things break.
We have forgotten that,
disenchanted;
amazed as children told
for the first time
how they were conceived.
Still the mind moves
continually west, following
paths beaten by the sun
risking ambush
and early darkness.
On Sundays, driving
past frontiers
lit by milkweed
let us find what wilderness
is left. Deep in the woods
it's possible to see the cruelties
between fox and rabbit
and their mutual beauty;
to study the creeks:
how the citizenry of small stones
is washed in waters that run
to the Potomac,
still clear in places,
in places muddy.
Today the river's a frozen slate,
a tabula rasa. It tempts us
as it did two hundred winters ago
to dare the dangerous
freedom
of the skater.

4. *depression*

Paperweight

Listen:
there is nothing
to hear.
The round world
is shaken with snow,
a thousand parachutes
settle—
they call the cold
a quiet death.
Our cells sign off
silently, like snowflakes
melting on the tongue,
and muffled white hoofs
ride us to sleep.

The Mirror: for Marvin Bell

The anguish of the fog
lies in dispersion;
and of the moon
in monotony
and the weight of the tides.
The anguish of the mulberry
sleeps while the silkworm sleeps.
You tell me nature is no mirror,
yet in the broken surface
of the lake I find
jagged pieces of my face.
Ask nature what love is.
Silence is answer enough.

The City

My mother calls it
"The City"
as if there were
no other,
and somewhere beneath
its sidewalks
a single subway car
ferries my father's ghost
across the Hudson.
My dreams remain
storefront dreams:
a bracelet of lights
circling my wrist,
stalagmites rising
1000 feet
in a cave
of streets.

Here in the country
the fanatic blue
of the sky
sends me indoors
where on clear nights
through the static
of insects sacrificed
against screens,
through the honking
of barnfowl
I pick up the siren call
of WNYC.

It Is Still Winter Here

I need no thermometer to tell me—
the rhododendrons are enough,
closed down like old umbrellas
all along the drive,
and your grandmother's voice from Florida
speaking of the weather there
as if the sun were some huge stone
rolled against the door of death
to hold it shut.
Here birds blaze briefly
at the window; a fox has died
under the deck, and we haul it away
our breath condensing into cartoon balloons
but ours have no words in them.
Even the trees seem no more than kindling—
so many dry sticks, and your grandmother's voice
crackling along the wire just now
like a brush fire soon to be put out.

Tourist

A Tintoretto angel
disguises itself in the curls
of my eldest child,
long grown to manhood.
A kneeling woman
is dressed in black;
her darkness reaches
all the way west,
back to the place I come from.
The few stars
are like loose change
in a strange currency.
Even as I write
these words
on a scrap of hotel paper
they look to my own eyes
as if I have translated them
from another
language.

Leaving Shangri-La

Remember Ronald Coleman
whom our mothers adored
and the delicate Asian girl
who was changed in a moment
into age itself:
her skin suddenly wrinkled
as slept-in linen,
her teeth loosening
in their sockets
like rows of burnt out
lightbulbs?

Well here they are
on the late show,
and it's all come true:
Coleman long dead;
the moon once plump
and shining
now hollow cheeked,
ready to pull the tide
like a hospital sheet
over our aging
faces.

Final

I studied
so long
for my life
that this morning when I waken
to it as if for the first time
someone is already walking
down the aisle
collecting the papers.

And indeed
all of the relevant blanks
have been filled in
with children lost
and found and lost again,
with meals served
and eaten
and cleared away.

Only one page
remains empty:
it is the hardest of all.
Its blanks are as white
as hospital corridors,
each of its question marks
is the shape
of a noose.

For I have been accused
of cheating, of writing
the same line
over and over again,
and once when I brushed my hair
sparks flew out
igniting
more than I intended.

Now is the time
for the shuffling of chairs,
the scribbling of excuses
on the margins. I did my best
but there were handicaps:
a low pain threshold,
so many words I couldn't choose
between them.

I studied
so long
for my life,
and all the time
morning had been parked
outside my window,
one wheel of the sun
resting against the curb.

Can so much light
be simply
to read by?
I open the curtain
to see,
just as the test
is over.

October Migrations

Are there more birds
than leaves
or are these black birds

the souls of leaves,
just as they fall
swarming to some leafy

heaven? My ears fill
with the crepe mourning
of wings which began

like that vague movement
in front of the eye
just as a migraine sets in.

Now a hundred birds
settle on one bare tree—
a candelabrum of crows

lighting the woods
into black flame. Soon
the smoke will begin.

25th High School Reunion

We come to hear the endings
of all the stories
in our anthology
of false starts:
how the girl who seemed
as hard as nails
was hammered
into shape;
how the athletes ran
out of races;
how under the skin
our skulls rise
to the surface
like rocks in the bed
of a drying stream.
Look! We have all
turned into
ourselves.

5. acceptance

Old Woman

In the evening
my griefs come to me
one by one.
They tell me what I had hoped to forget.
They perch on my shoulders
like mourning doves.
They are the color
of light fading.

In the day
they come back
wearing disguises.
I rock and rock
in the warm amnesia of sun.
When my griefs sing to me
from the bright throats of thrushes
I sing back.

Caroline

She wore
her coming death
as gracefully
as if it were a coat
she'd learned to sew.
When it grew cold enough
she'd simply button it
and go.

Consolations

Listen:
language does the best it can.
I speak

the dog whines
and in the changeling trees
late bees mumble, vague

as voices
barely heard
from the next room.

Later
the consolations
of silence.

The nights pass slowly.
I turn their heavy pages
one by one

licking my index finger
as my grandfather did
wanting to close the book on pain.

Afternoons smell of burning.
Already leaves have loosened
on the branch

small scrolls bearing
the old messages
each year.

You touch me—
another language. Our griefs
are almost one;

we swing them between us
like the child lent us awhile
who holds one hand of yours

and one of mine
hurrying us home

as street lights

start to flower
down the dark stem
of evening.

Geneticist

"I thought you were your father,"
someone said,
seeing for the first time
the blaze of curls around your neck
passed down by primogeniture,
though learned
from your own sons.
You spoke of how you used to hide
in a dim sanctuary
of women's shoes
against that father's drunken rage.
You sipped your scotch.

Now you learn the alphabet
of genes, study their silences,
the intricate switch
that turns them on and off
like lightbulbs on a hotel telephone
signalling: someone has left a message.
And the message itself intact
for generations—a letter
that has waited
in some dusty cubbyhole
delivered at last.
Open it!

Because

Because the night you asked me,
the small scar of the quarter moon
had healed—the moon was whole again;
because life seemed so short;
because life stretched before me
like the darkened halls of nightmare;
because I knew exactly what I wanted;
because I knew exactly nothing;
because I shed my childhood with my clothes—
they both had years of wear left in them;
because your eyes were darker than my father's;
because my father said I could do better;
because I wanted badly to say no;
because Stanley Kowalski shouted "Stella . . .";
because you were a door I could slam shut;
because endings are written before beginnings;
because I knew that after twenty years
you'd bring the plants inside for winter
and make a jungle we'd sleep in naked;
because I had free will;
because everything is ordained;
I said yes.

threads to be woven later

my grandmother's grave
like a loaf
of newly risen bread

my father's photograph
dying
in its frame

my mother
whose perfect beauty
I finally forgive

shades at the window
constellations
of dust

the tree of veins
a leaf
of my own blood

loving, being loved
the panicking
of the pulse

the weight
of the baby's head
fragile as a moon

a story
in my son's writing
the mother is the villain

the year
I took to my typewriter
as others take to their bed

words
leaking their meanings
ruining the page

the smell of the sea rising
the rising
of bread

postcard from cape cod

just now I saw
one yellow
butterfly
migrating
across buzzard's bay
how brave I thought
or foolish
like sending
a poem
across months
of silence
and on such
delicate
wings

Getting Down To Work

I clear my desk,
it is the only ordering I know:
friends to one side
the messages
they sent maybe weeks ago
travelling steadily like light from a star;
and on the other side bills
reminding me
I owe, I owe.

In the middle now this small, cleared space.

It is the same each morning,
the day opening
like the study window,
me leaning on the sill
Eve again:
the whole wide world
to choose from
(poet . . . cartographer)
where to go?

21st Anniversary

Last week
someone said
I had seer's eyes,
and you noticed their color
for the first time

though I have called myself
by your name
for exactly
as long
as by my father's.

It is a point
of no return. I cross it
to the sound of children laughing,
more dangerous
than children crying.

And all our dead animals
pass before my eyes:
the dogs more domestic
than either of us, fish
the color of greed.

Today in a clay pot
the Ponderosa Lemon hangs
in the east,
heavy and yellow.
You acknowledge it is morning

and turn to me.

You have learned
my combination by heart—
the safe flies open.
We are coming
of age.

love letter

it has snowed
on this page
and there are tracks
as of a small
animal lost
in the white weather

in the cold battle
of breath
yours forms
the only cloud
on which I can rest
my head

Arithmetic Lesson: Infinity

"In nature's infinite book of secrecy/a little I can read . . ."
William Shakespeare, *Antony and Cleopatra*

Picture a parade of numbers: 1
the sentry, out in front;
dependent, monogamous 2;
3 that odd man out, that 1 too many
always trying to break into line.
Numbers are subtracted, added
numbers fall by the way.
Some are broken into fractions—torn apart;
some assigned to stars, to crystals
of salt; to threads of water
on the ocean's dragging hem.
The proper numbers march together
their uniform buttons bright;
the rational numbers walk alone.
Every number on every clock repeats
its psalm over again
as minutes are numbered;
and children; and parcels of earth;
each sparrow as it falls;
each leaf after falling, before burning.
The negative numbers squabble
among themselves; imaginary numbers
count the number of kisses
that dance on the head of a pin.
And the parade goes on.
Each leaf of grass is numbered
just as it bends beneath
a numbered foot; each newt;
each spider's egg;
each grain of sleep caught
in each waking eye.
Pages are numbered as they turn;
dreams as they turn
into facts; the sun
as it rises on its fiery stalk
and as it sets.
But just as the end trembles into sight
the way the sea trembles
beyond the final dune
the steps of the marchers
grow smaller and smaller again—
the steps divide. Each number

hangs back, reluctant as a child
afraid of what he'll find
at the end of a darkened hall.
And though the destination
remains at hand
the parade moves slowly on: 1
the sentry, out in front;
dependent, monogamous 2;
3

The Five Stages of Grief

The night I lost you
someone pointed me towards
the Five Stages of Grief.
Go that way, they said,
it's easy, like learning to climb
stairs after the amputation.
And so I climbed.
Denial was first.
I sat down at breakfast
carefully setting the table
for two. I passed you the toast—
you sat there. I passed
you the paper—you hid
behind it.
Anger seemed more familiar.
I burned the toast, snatched
the paper and read the headlines myself.
But they mentioned your departure,
and so I moved on to
Bargaining. What could I exchange
for you? The silence
after storms? My typing fingers?
Before I could decide, *Depression*
came puffing up, a poor relation
its suitcase tied together
with string. In the suitcase
were bandages for the eyes
and bottles of sleep. I slid
all the way down the stairs
feeling nothing.
And all the time Hope
flashed on and off
in defective neon.
Hope was a signpost pointing
straight in the air.
Hope was my uncle's middle name,
he died of it.
After a year I am still climbing,
though my feet slip
on your stone face.
The treeline
has long since disappeared;
green is a color
I have forgotten.

But now I see what I am climbing
towards: *Acceptance*
written in capital letters,
a special headline:
Acceptance,
its name is in lights.
I struggle on,
waving and shouting.
Below, my whole life spreads its surf,
all the landscapes I've ever known
or dreamed of. Below
a fish jumps: the pulse
in your neck.
Acceptance. I finally
reach it.
But something is wrong.
Grief is a circular staircase.
I have lost you.